Feathers
A True Story.

by

Delpha R. Rockenbaugh

Edited and Illustrated by **Wendy Brantley**

Bloomington, IN  Milton Keynes, UK

auᴛʜᴏʀʜᴏᴜsᴇ®

AuthorHouse™
1663 Liberty Drive, Suite 200
Bloomington, IN 47403
www.authorhouse.com
Phone: 1-800-839-8640

AuthorHouse™ UK Ltd.
500 Avebury Boulevard
Central Milton Keynes, MK9 2BE
www.authorhouse.co.uk
Phone: 08001974150

First published by AuthorHouse 3/25/2007

ISBN: 978-1-4259-7689-7 (sc)

Printed in the United States of America
Bloomington, Indiana

This book is printed on acid-free paper.

Acknowledgements

This book is dedicated to my husband Thomas (Pops), who forgave me for being careless with our little feathered friend and was so patient with me while I wrote about the little bird we both loved so much.

Many thanks to Margaret Randall who encouraged me to write this book, gave me a book about a quail to get me started, and told me I could do it.

I want to give a special thank you to Wendy Brantley, a remarkable and gifted young lady, without whose talents for illustrating and editing this story would have been incomplete.

Thank you also goes to granddaughter D'Andra who typed the first copy.

Table of Contents

CHAPTER I
A NEW HOME

When God spoke the world into being, He must have been especially pleased to create the bird family. Such a variety of size and shape, color and personality! Many birds are highly prized for their color and plumage; others are valued for their loving natures, docile temperaments, and playful personalities. This is the story of Feathers - a remarkable little gray and white bird with a yellow head and bright orange circles on his cheeks. Feathers was a cockatiel.

Feathers began his life with a family of seven that lived in the state of Minnesota. The youngest daughter in the family received Feathers as a gift on her fifth birthday. No one realized then that the little girl was too young for such a bird friend. At feeding time, the girl would put on large black gloves because she was frightened by Feathers' pecking. She didn't know he was trying to talk to her, and what's more, Feathers was terrified by the big black gloves. Needless to say, Feathers and the little girl did not enjoy one another very much. The mother of the girl tried to help the bird feel more at home. She taught Feathers to kiss and to eat seeds she held in her teeth, and she taught him how to say, "Pretty bird."

Feathers faced another trial, worse than the big black gloves. Two boys, older brothers of the little girl, thought it funny to torment the pretty bird. One naughty fellow put ice cubes on top of Feathers' cage and when the ice began to melt, cold water dripped on Feathers' head. The other boy liked putting pencils through the cage bars so Feathers could not move around freely.

One day the family learned that through the father's job they were being transferred to Texas. No one minded moving, because in Texas they would be near the children's grandparents. So they packed the family van: father, mother, five children and their belongings, one large dog, a furry ferret, and Feathers. The mother, as a way of checking on Feathers, would call to him every hour or so; and from the very back of the van where his cage sat, Feathers would raise his sweet head and let her know he was still there.

About halfway to Texas the van broke down and Triple A was called for help. There was quite a wait for the truck, and on the side of the highway in a hot Kansas July, family and animals alike were getting pretty stressed. When at last a tow truck got the entire menagerie safely to Wichita, they were relieved to find next door to the repair shop a car dealership, where they were invited to wait. So five children, one large dog, a restless ferret, an overheated cockatiel, and a very stressed mother trooped over to the showroom, grateful for the air conditioning.

It wasn't too long before they all arrived in Fort Worth, Texas, and began looking for a new home. Instead of buying an existing house, they decided to build one. Meanwhile, the place they were staying was so small there was not room for Feathers cage, so Feathers was sent to live with the grandparents: Nona and Pops. What a blessing in disguise for two unsuspecting older people!

At first Nona and Pops were afraid of losing Feathers if he should want to fly away, so he spent a lot of time in his cage. Before long, however, the trio grew more comfortable in their new situation and Feathers received lots of attention - outside the cage. When Nona sat in her chair, Feathers enjoyed her lap and the good petting she gave him. Pops was the one to feed Feathers and to clean his cage.

After four months of waiting for the new house to be completed, the family moved in and made ready to get Feathers back. But a funny thing happened to change the course of Feathers' life. When Nona and Pops tried to take Feathers back to his family, Feathers fussed and made pleading noises, as if he did not want Nona and Pops to go. "Pretty bird. Pretty bird," he would say, and Nona hadn't the heart to leave him. After the fourth attempt to give Feathers back to his family, Nona and Pops resolutely left him and went home.

On the following evening, Pops needed an opportunity to talk with the father of the young and full family. While the two men visited, Nona went in to see Feathers, intending just to say hello and blow the chaff from his seed container. But to her surprise, there was none! Feathers had not touched his food for at least twenty-four hours.

Feathers begged to go home with Nona and Pops that evening, but they did not want to do anything until they had a chance to talk with their granddaughter. She had never really liked having a bird and told Nona and Pops

to take Feathers home. He could be their bird and she would visit him occasionally. The new arrangement suited everyone, and Nona happily tucked Feathers inside her jacket. The empty cage rode in the back of the truck and Pops, Nona, and Feathers started homeward. Now their home could permanently be home to this lovely and affectionate cockatiel.

Nona and Pops chose a convenient spot in the family room for the bird cage. They bought gourmet bird treats and made plans to never again clip Feathers' wings. Pops said, "He needs to feel and act like a bird." The old couple realized how much they already loved

Feathers and looked forward to their new life with him. Every day he did new things to make them laugh, and always he would step onto an extended finger when his cage door was opened. Always that is, until one day when Pops took him out to play and accidentally let go of the cage door, which dropped square onto the top of Feathers' little crested head. He never got on Pops' finger again!

CHAPTER II
LIFE WITH A COCKATIEL

When Feathers went to live with Nona and Pops, it changed their lives completely. They had added another member to their family and as a family member, Feathers was allowed to fly freely through the entire house. In this new living arrangement, Nona quickly discovered that it was a smart idea to keep wet paper towels handy for the bird droppings. She heard of a lady who had taught her own bird to do his business on a paper towel in the corner, but Nona didn't think she had the patience to potty train Feathers, so she did lots of cleaning.

Cockatiels are very curious animals and enjoy inspecting things all around them. One day Nona put an empty Fritos Puff sack on the floor beside her chair; Feathers soon discovered the sack and stepped inside. He sat in the sack for several minutes and rubbed his tiny tongue all around the inside surface.

That sack became one of his permanent toys, along with a necklace from Red Lobster, a wooden chew toy, and several other things which were kept for him on the floor in front of the fireplace. Sometimes Feathers would sleep inside the Fritos Puff sack for an hour or more. Nona only had to call his name to see the sack move a bit, and out he would come to be with her again.

Feathers was very protective of his toys. If Nona and Pops had a visitor who got too close to the toys, Feathers was on the move quick as a wink. Several people pulled back a hand bloodied by a firm bite from Feathers' sharp beak. Nona gave out Band-aids pretty often, until their friends learned their boundaries.

Feathers was especially protective of his sack and attacked the shoes of anyone who dared to walk too near it.

Pops had to learn his boundaries as well. Feathers did not like his boots. Many a fight ensued between Feathers and Pops' boots, complete with spread wings and tail and lots of bird screams. If Pops told him, "Okay, you won," Feathers would go on to something else, but always with a superior attitude. When the shoe repairman saw how Pops' boot had been cut through where the toe and sole met, he said, "You have a cockatiel!"

Besides the pile of toys in front of the fireplace, Feathers had his own little chair. It was a doll chair his first family had given him at Christmas, and it sat between Pops' and Nona's chairs in the family room. If Pops and Nona were in their chairs, Feathers was also in his. Cockatiels require a lot of sleep, so he took several naps a day, cozily perched on his chair near the ones he loved.

On Sunday nights after church, Nona always made popcorn. Before long, she and Pops discovered that Feathers enjoyed eating it with them. On many occasions, Feathers would even hop into the bowl and help himself to as much as he wanted.

One day Pops stopped by Feathers' cage and was talking to him about the cuttle bone that was in his cage. Small birds use cuttle bones to smooth the edges of their beaks and sharpen them a little, and it appeared that Feathers might need a new one. Pops only spoke about the bone; he didn't touch it or even motion toward it, but as he stepped away from the cage area and looked back over his shoulder, Feathers had gone straight to the bone and was rubbing his beak back and forth across it. Coincidence? Maybe it was - but Nona and Pops were convinced that Feathers could understand English, for things like this happened more often than they could explain.

Another day, Pops was in his office working and placed on his desk a small package of saltine crackers he'd found in his pocket. Feathers went in to visit, as he often did, and that day he discovered the crackers. Before Pops realized what was happening, Feathers proceeded to tear open the cellophane and eat most of the crackers, leaving a huge mess on the corner of Pops' desk.

A short time after Feathers went to live with Nona and Pops, the bird began to molt. There were small feathers and little bits of fluff everywhere. Feathers liked to be slick and smooth, so as the rough pinfeathers began to grow in, he would peck at them and pull some of them out. One such area, where he had pulled out a feather, became infected and was quite sore. It bothered the bird a lot and he would cry out in pain. Nona inspected him and found a sore the size of a nickel just above the left wing.

A call and an appointment were made to see a bird vet, who gave Nona and Pops a tube of ointment to put on Feathers. The sore didn't heal though because Feathers continued to pick at it. They called the vet again but he had stopped doctoring birds, so he recommended a colleague and recent graduate of Texas A&M University. This man put a plastic collar on Feathers so he could not turn his head back and peck at the wound, and gave Nona and Pops some liquid medication to give Feathers.

Well, the collar drove poor Feathers absolutely crazy! He ran and ran through the house and would not light anywhere. Twice he got on top of the refrigerator and both times he fell behind it. Nona and Pops were afraid he would get hurt so they finally took off the collar, hoping that the medicine alone would be sufficient. It did help for a while, but one Saturday afternoon Pops noticed that Feathers didn't seem to feel well. He was very quiet, and then suddenly he fell over.

As usual with doctors on a Saturday afternoon, finding a vet to treat Feathers was almost impossible. Finally they found a twenty-four hour clinic and fortunately, the doctor on duty was a bird doctor. Feathers was rushed into the clinic. After the doctor administered just two drops of some medicine, Feathers revived almost immediately and flew to her shoulder. He chirped and looked at the doctor as if he were telling her, "Thank you. I

like you!" Dr. Karen sent medicine home with them, and in a couple of weeks the wound finally healed.

After that incident, anytime Nona or Pops wasn't feeling well and went to lie on the sofa, Feathers would sit with the ailing one as if he were playing nursemaid. He missed Nona when she was in the hospital for a week one time. Pops stayed at the hospital all day with her, so Feathers spent a lot of time in his cage. In the evening when Pops returned and opened the cage, Feathers would sit on his shoulder, chatting in his ear, as if to ask all about Nona and how she was doing, and wishing for her speedy return.

Feathers loved to chew on things. Nona had decorated the kitchen cabinet tops with some wicker baskets. It didn't take long for Feathers, flying to the top of the cabinets on various occasions, to ruin several of the baskets. Whenever Nona made an arrangement of artificial flowers for the house, Feathers always found it and somehow managed to eat off all the leaves and flower petals. Nona was very unhappy with him. Feathers knew he was doing wrong, and when he saw her coming, he flew away and pretended to be innocent.

People who came to visit Nona and Pops had their share of his curious and active beak. Whoever happened to be wearing shoelaces usually got the plastic tips chewed off the shoe strings. The grandchildren had been taught to remove their shoes at the door, so Feathers went after their toes instead! Consequently, the kids always sat with their feet tucked underneath them.

At least once a week, Nona took Feathers into the shower with her. He sat on her finger underneath the spray of the water and enjoyed himself immensely. When he had had enough to feel clean, Feathers would fly out of the shower and preen himself perched on a swinging door that separated the commode area. If it was cold, Nona held him under the heat lamp to help him dry after she finished her shower.

Another pleasure for Feathers was Nona's closet. He always waited patiently atop the swinging door while Nona put on her make up, but as soon as she finished, off he went into the closet with her. While she selected her clothes for the day and began to dress, he would find the items that sparkled. He picked off sequins from blouses and beads from dresses or purses. Nona had to watch him very closely in the closet. One of her skirts had string beads dangling a little above the hemline and before she realized one day, Feathers had pulled off six strands of beads. Nona spent an afternoon repairing the damage and sewing the beads on again. But the next time she wore the skirt and lay down for a short nap on the sofa, Feathers discovered her sleeping and removed the bead strands once more.

There were times that Feathers went into the closet without Nona realizing it, and she went out and shut the door behind her. Noticing after a while that Feathers was missing, she would go through the house calling him. When he answered, she found him sitting very still in the darkness of her closet, waiting for the opening of the door. No matter where he was, Feathers always answered Nona's call, but he would never answer Pops.

In many ways Feathers was like a child. He was not allowed in the front entry hall on the Oriental rug. Sometimes he would walk across the family room from playing with his toys and start toward the entry hall. Nona would tell him 'NO" and he would stop and look around at her. If she looked away, he would start into the hall again. Nona would say, "NO FEATHERS." He would look at her and go back into the family room in resignation. Upon occasion he did get all the way into the hall without being noticed, but before long he was back where he belonged looking for something to do.

Feathers was a constant companion to Nona, so when she went to the kitchen to prepare a meal, Feathers was usually there also. His favorite seat, when he was not on her shoulder, was on top of the refrigerator, and from that vantage point he could observe all Nona's activity. The pantry was beside the refrigerator, and when Nona opened the pantry door, Feathers would look at her through the crack between the pantry door and the cabinet. He would alternately lay his head against the side of the cabinet and then look at Nona through the crack. She would say, "Peek-a-boo," and Feathers would again lay his head back and then look at her through the crack. This became a favorite game during kitchen duties.

Sometimes while Nona was cooking, Feathers walked around the kitchen floor, and she took great care not to step on him. Feathers discovered his shadow on the refrigerator door and had lots of fun watching it. If Nona had to step outside a moment, she would put Feathers back on the refrigerator and tell him, "I'll be back, I'll be back." Feathers waited for her exactly where she left him. He was easy to keep track of up there, but once in a while he would disappear into a drawer that was left open. Nona unknowingly closed him into the silverware drawer one day and he patiently awaited her rescue.

Feathers ate his meals at the same time as Nona and Pops. Often they took their food on TV trays to the family room where they watched the news while they ate. Feathers liked to check out what Pops was eating and sat boldly on Pops' TV tray. He usually tasted the food as well, but didn't care much for people food. When Nona carried her tray into the family room to eat her meal, Feathers would walk along beside her, just as a puppy would do. It was so amusing to Nona for him to be running along with her, as fast as his tiny legs could go.

After supper and kitchen cleanup, Nona would often do some kind of handwork in the evenings while Pops dozed in his chair. Feathers was never far away in giving his own special assistance to Nona's projects. After helping her a while however, Feathers often ended up in Pops' lap, the two fellows napping together for the remainder of the evening.

CHAPTER III
FLYING FREE

When Nona arose each morning a couple of hours after Pops, she would take the cover from Feathers' cage and wish him 'good morning'. As soon as Nona opened the cage, Feathers would step onto her finger and come out for his morning kiss. During that part of their ritual, Feathers was cupped inside Nona's hands, but after his kiss he loved to ride around the house on Nona's shoulder.

Neither Nona nor Pops was a morning person, so not much was said until after nine o'clock. Feathers fit into the morning routine very well and also remained quiet until mid-morning. After breakfast Feathers helped with Nona's household tasks. Whether it was kitchen cleaning or bedmaking, Feathers was always right there. Nona did the work; he sat on her shoulder. Sometimes he flew to the top of the bedroom etagere to observe her work. Sometimes he would go under the sofa and bite the edges off old magazines that were put there just for this purpose. These were the calm parts of a day in their new life, but not everyday was quite so peaceful.

Pops and Nona lived in a rural area that was also home to lots of squirrels, many kinds of birds, raccoons, opossum, and even a gray fox. The animals and their antics provided a constant source of entertainment, and they got lots of food from the two kind people. One day a startling thing happened. Pops was away for the day and Nona was talking with a friend on the telephone. Feathers, as usual, was on Nona's shoulder. As she visited she noticed the neighbor's cat coming across the yard toward the bird feeder. The cat often killed the birds, but this time Nona set out to stop it.

She ran to the front door, phone in hand, and forgetting about Feathers on her shoulder, she opened the door and went out. She clapped her hands and yelled at the cat. Scat! The sudden noise startled Feathers and he flew up and away. Feeling sick at the realization of what had happened, Nona told her friend on the phone to hold on and she began walking toward the backyard - the direction that Feathers had flown. Over and over she could

hear Feathers calling: "Pretty bird! Pretty bird! Pretty bird!"

Nona found Feathers sitting on the rock wall at the back of the yard where lots of trees grew. When she called his name, he flew towards her and landed at the edge of a flowerbed. Nona picked him up and with great relief, returned him to the house. Nona's friend on the phone said that was the most excitement she had had in quite a while.

Feathers flew off a second time when Nona joined Pops in the yard to discuss a flowerbed. Feathers was so often on Nona's shoulder that it was natural for her to walk around with him and not even realize he was there. So again, she forgot he might need to stay behind when she needed to go outside. And again, a loud noise scared Feathers. He flew so high he could barely be seen and Nona and Pops were worried they would never see him again. But he landed in a neighbor's tree next door and began his 'pretty bird' call. Pops got a ladder from the garage and Nona started climbing. Feathers was twenty feet off the ground and couldn't seem to maneuver down the branches well enough for Nona to reach him. With the help of a long pole, Pops finally got Feathers low enough for Nona to reach him, and she brought him the rest of the way down.

The third time Feathers flew away had to do with the neighbor's cat again. A man had come to talk to Nona and Pops about new windows for their house. Nona looked out a window, saw the cat coming, and out she jumped to chase away the cat. This time Feathers flew into a large live oak tree in the front yard. Out came the ladder again to be able to reach him and make the rescue.

When Feathers had lived with Nona and Pops for about three years, Nona went out in the yard before Christmas to gather some greenery for an arrangement. She heard Pops call out, "Is Feathers with you?" She realized he was sitting on her shoulder as always, but that if she answered loud enough for Pops to hear, it might startle Feathers into flying. So she said nothing. She slowly turned and calmly walked back into the house and put Feathers on top of the refrigerator. He liked to sit up there while she was outside, and whew! was she glad to put him there this time!

Several months later Feathers had another nice flight. Nona had stepped out the back of the house to get the hummingbird feeder for a nectar refill. She had done it many times with Feathers on her shoulder, but something evidently startled him this time, for as soon as she stepped outside, Feathers flew. He made two large circles around the house, but as he came around the second time, Nona walked out the front door and said firmly, "Feathers, come here." He landed in the flowerbed at her feet and into the house they went. He was always glad to get back inside, but he also seemed quite proud of his flying achievements.

CHAPTER IV
TRAVELING

Nona and Pops enjoyed traveling and going places, and did so rather often. Whenever they were able to do so, they took Feathers with them. So he began to enjoy traveling very much as well. When the happy bird had an opportunity to go, he rode along in an old purse of Nona's. The purse was made of gold mesh and had a drawstring top. Nona had almost thrown it away once during closet cleaning because it was getting worn, but the thought came to her it would make a good travel bag for Feathers. It was roomy enough, and the mesh let in plenty of air, and of course cockatiels love sparkly objects. After a while, whenever Feathers saw Nona bring out the purse, he knew he would get to go along on whatever journey they had planned for the day.

A couple of times Feathers went with Nona and Pops to the Fort Worth Home and Garden

Show. On their first trip, the show featured a section of animals which they decided to visit. When Nona showed Feathers riding in his purse to the other spectators, they were enthralled. Later, one lady, who had seen Feathers, tracked down Nona and Pops in that huge convention center so she could show her husband the lovely bird in the gold bag.

Three years later the trio again visited the Home and Garden Show and were there for five hours. Feathers was quite content just to be with them and never let out a cheep. When he needed a drink, Nona would take him out of the bag and hold him up to a water fountain for him to take refreshment. He did not like drinking out of a dish, but he loved the fountain water coming out fresh for him to drink.

Nona and Pops had a niece whose husband made Feathers a special feeding box for their trips. The box was twelve inches square and had a ladder and a jingle bell on it. Pops would set the box on the floorboard between himself and Nona and that was where Feathers ate when they traveled. There was also a water dish on the feeding box, but Feathers refused to drink from it. He waited until each rest stop for Nona to find him a fountain and hold him up to

drink. The people nearby were always amused at the pair.

If Nona and Pops went out of town overnight, Pops had to make sure of each motel before he made their reservations. Some motels did not allow pets - not even little birds. When they arrived and were assigned to a room, Nona always turned back the bedspread and blanket first, then turned back the sheet over them. It made for an easier cleanup if Feathers should happen to soil the sheets.

Feathers loved to stay in motel rooms. It was cozy and he enjoyed sleeping in the same room with Nona and Pops. If they stayed more than one night, Feathers like watching the maids when they came to clean the room.

The maids thought it was fun to talk to the pretty bird. It was an unusual sight for them. Sometimes they brought extra rags to the room in case Nona had to do any clean up of Feathers' little messes. But Nona always brought her own rags as well. She always made sure on check-out day that no bird seed was left behind. She carried along a small sweeper so there would be no sign left that a bird had been there.

When Nona and Pops traveled during the cooler seasons and mealtime came around, they would leave Feathers in the car with the window slightly cracked for air and go to eat in a restaurant. They always assured him first by saying, "We'll be back." And when they did

return, they found Feathers waiting for them on top of his cage or perched on the steering wheel. If, on the other hand, they traveled in the heat of the summer, Nona and Pops would just buy sandwiches to go. Feathers was happier with that choice because that way, the trio was together at mealtime.

As they traveled around, Feathers sometimes rode on top of his cage, which was taken along for the bird's sleeping quarters in a motel room. More often, however, Feathers rode on Nona's ankle, down low where the sun would not shine on him so brightly. As darkness came on those driving days, he would gradually make his way upward to Nona's chest where he could safely nestle under her chin. He was comfortable and she delighted to cuddle with him as he settled down for the night.

Feathers made quite an impression on people as they were out and about. In a trip to Arizona one summer, Nona and Pops took him out and the three of them went shopping. As Feathers rode around in his gold purse, he was usually quiet and observant. If he let out a chirp now and then, people would look up, thinking that a bird had somehow gotten into the store. That day a couple of pretty, young store clerks took an interest in Feathers. Nona took him out of the gold purse and they visited with the clerks a while. Eventually the girls needed to get back to work, but assured Nona and Pops that Feathers had made their day!

Shopping at Toys 'R Us for the grandchildren one Christmastime, Nona, Pops and Feathers were following a clerk who was helping them to locate a particular item. When Feathers let out a rather loud chirp, the girl looked at Nona and asked, "Was that you?" Nona and Pops got a good laugh as Nona showed the girl the mesh bag with Feathers inside. The girl proceeded to draw the attention of many more shoppers to that pretty bird in the gold purse.

Sometimes it was impossible for Feathers to go on a trip with Nona and Pops, and on those occasions, he stayed with his original family, Nona and Pops' children and grandchildren. When it came time for them to leave, Nona and Pops had to assure Feathers, "We'll be back. We'll be back," for him to be content. When they returned, Feathers was unbelievably happy and would begin screeching before they even got into the house. Then he would chatter at the old couple all the way home; his voice would rise and fall as if he was relaying to them everything that happened to him while they were gone. Once the great grandchildren had been there and at the end of Feathers' narrative, he let out two especially loud screeches. It made Nona and Pops wonder if he was accusing those children of something.

The children and grandchildren had stories to tell about Feathers as well. They had a large dog and while Feathers was staying with them, the dog was frequently reminded to leave the bird alone. How could they have known that Feathers would take full advantage of the dog? As the dog lay quietly under the table one day, Feathers went under also and began to peck the dog on the nose. The poor dog lay still and just looked sadly at his persecutor.

Another time Nona and Pops went to pick up Feathers at the children's house and were promptly informed by their daughter that Feathers had eaten a diamond out of a new pair of earrings while he was sitting on her shoulder. They all searched for a long time, but the diamond was never found.

After some of their longer trips when Feathers had stayed behind, he refused to sleep by himself in the family room at night. In his cage he would chirp and make all sorts of noises as if he was afraid they were going to leave again. To relieve the bird's fear, Pops would take the cage into their bedroom, and when Feathers could see them again, he would quiet down and go to sleep. Only if he could spend that first night back home in their room and be with them all the next day, would Feathers then be content to sleep the second night back in the family room by himself.

There were times Feathers knew he was about to be put into his cage for a while and when Nona came for him, like a little child he would run away as fast as his tiny legs could carry him, and hide under a chair or coffee table. With difficulty Nona would capture him and soothe him and try to make him understand the situation. If Nona and Pops needed to go erranding, it took several "Good-byes" and "We'll be backs" before Feathers seemed to know that everything would be okay. His running away under furniture often happened on Saturday evenings, for then Nona and Pops went to bed at eleven o'clock instead of their usual midnight bedtime. Their purpose to make Sunday morning church attendance easier with an extra hour of sleep was often defeated by an ornery little bird who had to be chased about the house before he would consent to go to bed. But oh, how they loved their little bird!

CHAPTER V
KISSES AND GROCERY SACKS

So many quaint and interesting things filled the lives of Nona and Pops while Feathers was around. One of the earliest things they discovered in the realm of bird affection was that Feathers loved to kiss. Nona only had to say, "Kiss," and pucker up her lips and Feathers would kiss as long as she would stay. If she worked around the house and happened to pass Feathers perching somewhere, she would lean over him and get a little kiss on her way by. Feathers was definitely the jealous sort when it came to Nona and how she gave or received affection. Whenever Pops hugged Nona or wanted to give her a kiss, Feathers would fly to Nona's shoulder and put his head in between them.

Nona and Pops were surprised and delighted to learn that Feathers liked music - <u>good</u> music. They determined the fact during the first Christmas season with their little feathered friend. Nona was sitting in her recliner watching a Christmas program that featured a lot of classical music. Feathers flew over to see what was happening and became very interested in the music as he sat on the toe of Nona's shoe. If the music changed to pop or rock and roll, Feathers would shake his head up and down and fuss until Nona turned off the offending tune.

Like most animals, birds have an ability to sense danger and in particular, the danger of fire. Feathers always accompanied Nona into the kitchen so as she cooked, she had to watch Feathers closely, lest he land on the stove and burn himself. He never went close to the burner and Nona assumed he could sense the danger. The strange thing was, his cautions did not extend to the fireplace.

In fact, Feathers loved the fireplace - especially when it contained a burning fire. When Pops would lay a fire, Feathers would fly to the hearth and warm himself in front of the dancing flames. One mild day when no fire was burning, Feathers flew to the hearth to make his opinion known. He walked up and down, back and forth, alternately peering into the firebox and

looking over his shoulder at Pops until he got what he wanted. Pops built him a fire.

One day Pops and Nona were gone for several hours, and upon their return, they opened Feathers' cage and spoke to him the way they always did. He got on top of his cage and began some very insistent fussing. His fussing and squawking went on for fifteen minutes or more, and Nona said, "I think someone was here while we were gone and he's trying to tell us about it." Pops agreed and they went to the front door, opened it, and discovered to their surprise that someone had indeed been there. The UPS man had left them a package while they were gone.

Another time, Nona and Pops were talking in the kitchen and Feathers was on his cage in the family room. Suddenly, Feathers began making an excited and funny noise. As Nona went to check on him, the UPS delivery man came up to the front door. Nona and Pops grinned at each other and were thankful for a little 'watch bird' to look out for them.

During times of relaxation, when Pops sat in his big arm chair, Feathers would climb onto his lap or perhaps sit on the chair back behind him. To go from the lap to the back of the chair, Feathers used the arms of the chair as his walkway. If Pops' arms were in his way, Feathers would give him a little peck to let him know he wanted to go by. When that was accomplished and he had settled onto the back of the chair, he and Pops usually took their naps. If Pops had to leave the chair for some reason, Feathers would wait patiently for his return.

At the lunch hour, Nona and Pops each prepared their own food. While they worked, Feathers frequently occupied the kitchen floor between their feet. It was not the safest place for such a little fellow, and he often got scooted across the floor or had his tail stepped on. Depending on how hard he got bumped, Feathers always let out a chirping cry that matched the offense.

Nona and Pops ate their lunch on trays so they could watch the twelve o'clock news. When they got to the family room with their lunch plates, Feathers would get on the lamp table between the old couple and stare at Pops until a place was prepared for him as well. Then Feathers would hop over to Pops' tray and eat his lunch right alongside Nona and Pops.

Several things were discovered that were not at all to Feathers liking. For one, he hated the sound of the doorbell. To accommodate him, Nona or Pops, upon seeing the arrival of a visitor, would try to get to the door before the person had a chance to ring the bell. When it did ring, Feathers would fly nervously around all over the house until Nona could find and console him. Nor did Feathers like the noise of a vacuum. On cleaning day, he would only be

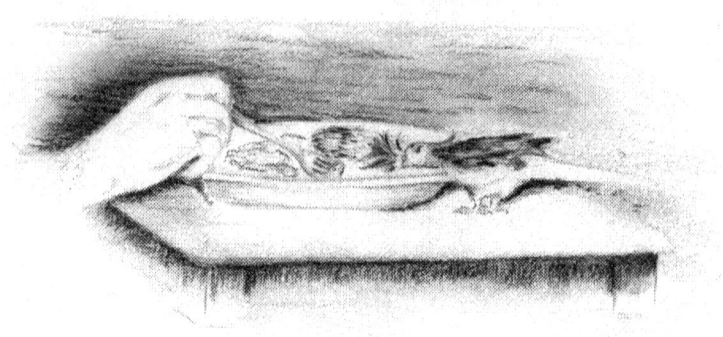

content sitting safely on Nona's shoulder until the vacuum was turned off and put away.

Another thing that bothered Feathers was being outside too long. If work was needed in the flower beds, Nona tried to make it a special outing for him by taking him outside in his cage, setting the cage on the soft, green grass, and sliding out the floor of the cage. In this way, she thought he could enjoy the coolness and interesting texture of the grass. But not Feathers! Not only did he dislike the grass, he also did not like to hear the wild birds chirping from high in the trees. Feathers would sit up on the perch inside his cage and chirp loudly, as if he were trying to drown out the sounds of the other birds. He was always relieved when quitting time came.

Having company was not particularly fun for Feathers either. Maybe it was jealousy or maybe it was only that to Feathers' way of thinking, the happy trio were sufficient unto themselves. He would try to behave patiently when visitors came, although his intense stare didn't deceive Nona. Upon the departure of the visitors, it was obvious that Feathers was most contented and happy when he was home alone with his Nona and Pops.

Feathers was such a source of wonder and delight to the old couple. On grocery shopping day, Pops always brought in the grocery sacks and set them on the counter to be unloaded. Feathers self-appointed job was to perch on the edge of each sack in its turn and inspect the contents of every one. He looked like a little child going through the new groceries to see if anything especially delicious had been brought home just for him. That always made Nona laugh.

In the evening before bedtime, Nona and Pops liked to play a few hands of a card game. Feathers did not want to be left out, so before they began their game, he would jump to the middle of the table, pick up a few cards with his beak, and throw them back over his head. After that he would eat a few squares of Chex cereal (Pops' favorite card-playing snack) and then perch on Nona's ankle until the games were finished. If the card games went on too long for Feathers' satisfaction, Nona and Pops were subjected to his fussing reprimand from under the table. When they did finish playing, Nona would pick up the cards and say, "Come on, Feathers. Let's go to bed," whereupon, the tired little bird would hop over to the base of his cage and wait to be put to bed. Nona would pick him up off the floor, kiss him goodnight, and put him in the cage. He sat on his perch waiting for his cage to be covered, but if Nona and Pops did not both bid him goodnight, he fussed and refused to go to sleep until they had both spoken to him. "Goodnight, Feathers." "Goodnight, Feathers."

CHAPTER VI
THE FINAL TRIP

One fall season, Nona and Pops took a trip and Feathers did not get to go. Nona had invited her brother and sister-in-law to spend a week with them at a nice resort. The resort had told them, "Absolutely, No Pets," and gave the reason that people with allergies reacted to the bird dander. Nona and Pops resented the hypocrisy behind their reasoning, knowing that the resort gave smokers complete freedom to damage the air quality. But the trip was planned, and so they went. Who could have known that but a few days into the trip, Nona's brother would have an allergic reaction to the smoke residue in their room. He awoke one morning to the realization that his eyes were almost swollen shut, and the vacationing foursome had to leave and cut the vacation a couple of days short..

Having arrived back in town, Nona and Pops picked up Feathers at their daughter's house and took him home. Although Feathers seemed glad to see them, something appeared to be wrong with him. He behaved unusually that night, and the next morning he would not get out of his cage and refused to eat his breakfast. As the day went on, Nona and Pops became concerned: this sad little fellow did not act like their normally happy cockatiel.

On the following day, Nona proposed a trip to the vet's office. Dr. Karen examined Feathers thoroughly and finally asked if Nona and Pops had been on a trip without him. When they told her of their recent resort visit, she said that Feathers was suffering from separation anxiety disorder, and prescribed Prozac for him. She showed them how to administer the medication, and Nona and Pops gave it to him

faithfully each morning. Feathers soon showed much improvement and was happy and content once more.

Then came a very wonderful day for Feathers as Nona took him from the cage and put him into the gold purse. Oh joy! He got to go along with them this time. The three were headed toward Big Bend National Park. Nona had never been there and Pops wanted very much for her to see the area where he had worked many years before. He was excited himself to see what changes had occurred since he had been there. And Feathers - he didn't care where they went as long as they could all go together.

So into the truck went luggage, a bird cage, Feathers' feedbox, wet paper towels, and extra water. Preparations were not many because they only intended to be gone a few days. In the truck Feathers had three favorite places to perch: on the top of his cage, on Nona's ankle, and in Nona's lap. The lap was really his preference because Nona would always pet and stroke him. He especially loved having her rub backwards on his head and crest and he would drop his head, shut his eyes, and sit very still as long as she would pet him. That kind of treatment, not to mention riding in the car for hours, made Feathers sleepy and he would begin to yawn. He yawned, and he yawned, six times, eight times. Oh, how Nona and Pops would laugh to see that tiny beak on the colorful little face going back and forth, open and shut, with each successive yawn.

The first day they traveled about four hundred miles and decided to stop for the night in Fort Stockton, Texas. They checked into a motel room and got Feathers settled and fed. He was so happy to be there with the two people he loved most. The next morning Pops prepared for the day's travel while Nona gave Feathers his Prozac. She could tell by Feathers' expression that he felt great and was very cheerful that day.

Pops finished loading the truck and told Nona and Feathers to get in the truck and he would be back shortly. Nona got her gold purse and Feathers hopped right into it, knowing that the three of them were going to ride together again that day. When they got into the truck, Nona let Feathers out of the gold purse and settled him on her lap for their travel. She looked down at her hands and noticed that her rings were missing. She thought she had put them in one of the suitcases, but decided

44

to check the motel room once more to make sure she had not left them.

Quite often Nona carried Feathers tucked inside her vest, and since he was already out of his bag, she quickly slipped him into her sweater and turned to get out of the truck. But as she stepped out, a very terrible thing happened! The truck had been parked next to a pillar, which prevented Nona from seeing the curb, so that as she got out of the truck and started back into the motel, she fell. Feathers was frightened in the fall and flew out of her sweater and straight up into the air. As Nona lay face down on the sidewalk, she could hear the sound of Feathers' wings becoming more and more faint.

The motel was surrounded by trees on three sides, and Nona tried to believe that Feathers would land in one and wait for her there. She got up with a bleeding face and a smarting hand, but all she could think of was Feathers. She and Pops walked all around the motel searching and calling, but Feathers did not answer. He always answered her calls at home, but what was wrong this time?

Nona's face was swelling and her hand was hurting badly, but she didn't want to leave. After much urging from Pops, Nona did finally go to the hospital. The emergency room doctor put seven stitches in her eyelid, splinted a broken finger, and cleaned up her other scrapes. But as soon as he finished, Nona insisted on trying the search again for her dear bird. She and Pops drove back to the motel and walked the entire property several times over calling and calling for Feathers. No sound was heard from him and their hearts began to sink.

Because of Nona's injuries, Pops thought they should go back home. Sadly and reluctantly they drove the four hundred miles back to Fort Worth, but the next day, depressed by the thought that no one else would be looking for Feathers, they drove to Fort Stockton once more to renew the search. That night Nona could not sleep for thinking of a lonely little cockatiel, hungry and cold, wondering where his people were. In a light dozing sleep, Nona dreamed Feathers came back and landed happily on her shoulder. But it was only a dream.

A new idea came the next morning that brought Nona and Pops some hope. The hotel clerk described a local morning radio program that would freely advertise items or events for people in the community. So off they went to the radio station to report their loss and post a reward. After that they visited the police department, but the animal control officer said he didn't have a good way to catch birds. Nona assured him that if he could just help them find Feathers, she would catch him herself.

Nona and Pops walked the fields near the motel where Feathers was last seen. The fields were full of cactus, creosote bushes, weeds of all sorts, small trees- but no Feathers. They knocked on doors in the surrounding neighborhood. They went to stores and places of business. They visited a nearby truck stop, imagining the truck drivers swapping stories of unusual things they had seen. But no one had seen Feathers. No one had seen the little gray bird with the pretty yellow head and the round orange cheeks. No one had seen him.

All the while they searched, Nona kept thinking of her frightened little friend who did not like being outside, did not like other birds, and did not like the bright sun. She knew that if he was alive, he was a very unhappy little fellow, and on that morning she had last seen him, he had been so cheerful.

Nona and Pops contacted two veterinary clinics in hopes that if someone found Feathers, he might be taken in for an

examination. They called the newspaper office in Fort Stockton and put in an advertisement offering a reward of fifty dollars to anyone who found Feathers and took him to one of the clinics. Nona posted a letter in the newspaper describing their sad adventure in Fort Stockton, hoping that someone in the town might be able to help them.

Back in Fort Worth, Nona and Pops were depressed and lonely for their little feathered friend. Nona jumped at every ring of the phone and carefully searched the mail each day. But there never came a call or a response to her letter. All Nona and Pops could say in their sadness was, "Feathers...you didn't come back."

The story of Feathers is true, and though Nona and Pops have another cockatiel named Kandy, they still miss Feathers very much and wanted to share the account of his life with others.

About the Author

Delpha R. Rockenbaugh is mother and step-mother to four children. She and her husband have ten grandchildren and eight great-grandchildren.

Mr. and Mrs. Rockenbaugh live in a rural area where they have a lot of wild animals and birds and keep food out for them.

Del has no credentials as an author. Her claim to books is that she has been a reader all her life and does enjoy reading.

Most of her spare time is spent with handwork. She enjoys doing counted cross stitch and enters a project every year in a money raising event to give scholarships to young people who need help to attend college.

When Del worked, she was a secretary and typist. Now she stays busy with children, travel, and her church. She lives in Willow Park, Texas with her husband, Thomas, and a new cockatiel named Kandy.